HUMMINGBIRDS
IN THE GARDEN

HUMMINGBIRDS IN THE GARDEN

By Roma Gans   Illustrated by Grambs Miller

THOMAS Y. CROWELL COMPANY   NEW YORK

Editors: *DR. ROMA GANS,* Professor Emeritus of Childhood Education, Teachers College, Columbia University

DR. FRANKLYN M. BRANLEY, Chairman of The American Museum—Hayden Planetarium, consultant on science in elementary education

MANUFACTURED IN THE UNITED STATES OF AMERICA

L.C. Card 69-11083

1   2   3   4   5   6   7   8   9   10

HUMMINGBIRDS IN THE GARDEN

LET'S READ AND FIND OUT

A ruby-throated hummingbird is very little. It is only three and a half inches long and weighs less than one penny. But it can fly five hundred miles without stopping.

TEXAS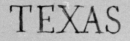

LOUISIANA

MISSISSIPPI

GULF

OF

MEXICO

MEXICO

YUCATAN

BRITISH HONDURAS

GUATEMALA

Some hummingbirds fly all the way across the Gulf of Mexico each spring. They fly from Central America to the United States. The male arrives first. The female comes about a week later. Maybe they fly to your yard.

The male is bright in color. His throat is red like
rubies. The female's throat is not bright; but she
too is called a ruby-throated hummingbird.

They are called hummingbirds but they do not hum or sing. Their wings make a humming sound when they fly. They can beat their wings sixty times in one second—over three thousand times in one minute! The wings beat so fast you can see only a blur.

No other birds can fly the way hummingbirds do. They can fly straight up in the air, then dart here and there in a zigzag. They can stay in the same place in the air without going up or down, forward or backward. They can hover over a flower the way a helicopter hovers over a building. Their wings keep beating fast while they hover. A hummingbird can even fly backward. No other bird can fly in so many ways.

The hummingbird has stronger wings for its size than any other bird. The wings are fastened to the shoulders so they can swing around easily.

A hummingbird can tilt its wings. It can tilt them up and back. It can flip them over so the underside points toward the sky. Its wings work like helicopter propellers.

A hummer can dive straight down at an enemy. It can go in and out, up and down. It flits and darts. It can drive away a big crow, a hawk, or a blue jay.

How can such a small bird fly so fast without getting tired? You get tired if you swing your arms up and down just a few times. The muscles in the wings of a hummingbird are strong. The bird breathes very fast, and its heart beats fast, too.

It eats all day long. You eat three times a day. A hummingbird must eat fifty to sixty times a day.

Your body temperature is a little more than 98
degrees. A hummingbird's temperature is about
113 degrees. At night, while the bird is sleeping
and not eating, its temperature drops. It may go
as low as 65 degrees.

When the hummingbird's temperature is this low, the bird is barely alive. We say it is *torpid*. When the sun rises and the day brightens, the hummingbird wakes up. It eats right away, and its temperature goes up right away. Then it can again fly, dart, and dive.

Hummingbirds find their food in flowers that hold nectar. They find nectar in lilies, morning glories, honeysuckle, and nasturtiums.

Nectar is sweet like sugar and water, or like honey and water. Nectar gives hummingbirds strength at once. It gives them quick energy.

Hummingbirds have a long thin beak. They can reach nectar deep inside a flower. They suck up the nectar through a long tongue inside the beak. The tongue is hollow like a soda straw.

The sugar in nectar is a food the hummingbirds
need. Often small insects are caught in the sticky
nectar. The hummingbird eats them, too. They
are the meat in their meals.

Hummingbirds get all their food while flying or hovering. Other birds can perch, swim, or walk while they eat. The hummingbird cannot walk. It uses its feet only to hold onto a twig when it rests.

You can watch a hummingbird eat if you sit very still. First it dives down and stops in front of the flower. Then it hovers. While the bird hovers, its wings are beating fast. It darts its long thin beak into the flower. It sucks up the nectar. Quickly it flies backwards away from the flower. It hovers, then flies to another flower.

Hummingbirds seem to like the color red. They dart at red flowers even if the flowers have no nectar. They may even fly at a red ribbon tied onto a tree.

Tie one to a branch and see if a hummer will fly
at it.

Hummingbirds will come back year after year to the same garden. You can make a feeder for them. Use a small bottle about three inches tall. The bottle must have a wide mouth. Color the upper part of the bottle red. Use nail polish or red tape. The red color helps the hummingbird notice the feeder.

Wrap string around the feeder and tie it to the branch of a tree four or five feet from the ground.

RECIPE

1

2

24

Now make the nectar. Mix a spoonful of sugar and
two spoonfuls of hot water. Fill the feeder with
the sugar water. Be sure it is brimful.

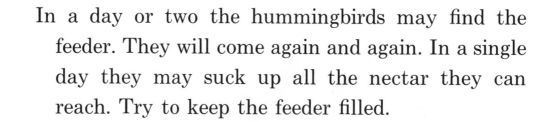

In a day or two the hummingbirds may find the feeder. They will come again and again. In a single day they may suck up all the nectar they can reach. Try to keep the feeder filled.

Bugs and dust may spoil the nectar after three or four days. Every few days wash the feeder and put in new nectar.

The hummingbird hunts for good eating places as soon as it comes north. Put your feeder out when flowers start to bloom. Be sure to keep nectar in the feeder all the time, right up to the end of summer.

Hummingbirds need nectar so they can beat their wings fast. They need nectar so they can zigzag in the air, dive-bomb at a crow, and hover in front of flowers.

NORTH AMERICA

ATLANTIC OCEAN

GULF OF MEXICO

CENTRAL

AMERICA

PACIFIC OCEAN

PANAMA CANAL

SOUTH AMERICA

At the end of summer food in flowers is hard to find.
But that's when the hummingbirds need food the
most. They need food to get ready for the long
flight back to their winter home in Central
America.

ABOUT THE AUTHOR

Roma Gans has called children "enlightened, excited citizens." She believes in the fundamental theory that children are eager to learn and will whet their own intellectual curiosity if they are encouraged by and provided with stimulating teachers and materials.

Dr. Gans received her B.S. from Columbia Teachers College and her Ph.D. from Columbia University. She began her work in the educational field in the public schools of the Middle West as a teacher, supervisor, and assistant superintendent of schools. She is Professor Emeritus of Childhood Education at Teachers College, Columbia University, and lectures extensively throughout this country and Canada.

Dr. Gans is vitally interested in nature and all its phenomena. She has many bird-feeding stations at her house in West Redding, Connecticut, where she watches birds and their habits. She enjoys living in the country where she can observe the changing seasons of the year.

ABOUT THE ILLUSTRATOR

A pair of hummingbirds darting around a weigela bush delighted Grambs Miller as she worked on the illustrations for this book. The weigela bush is planted in the garden of her summer home on Martha's Vineyard, Massachusetts.

Born in Peking, China, where her grandfather was a missionary, Mrs. Miller came to the United States with a scholarship to the Art Students League in New York City. She studied there with Harry Sternberg, George Grosz, Thomas Hart Benton, and John Steuart Curry. Mrs. Miller's drawings were exhibited in Peking, Shanghai, and Hong Kong before she came to the United States and have received a citation for merit from the Society of Illustrators. She is the illustrator of many cookbooks and books for children. Mrs. Miller and her husband spend their winters in New York.